My first Picture book

ENGLISH ARABIC

250 words of everyday life

This book belongs to :

....

....

خ Ḫāʾ (kha)	ح Ḥāʾ (haa')	ج Ǧīm (G)	ث Ṯāʾ (thā')	ت Tāʾ (T)	ب Bāʾ (B)	ا ʾAlif (A)
ص Ṣād	ش šīn (ch)	س sīn (S)	ز Zāy (Z)	ر Rāʾ (R)	ذ Ḏāl (dhāl)	د Dāl (D)
ق Qāf (Q)	ف Fāʾ (F)	غ Ġayn (gh)	ع ʿAyn	ظ Ẓāʾ (Zaa')	ط Ṭāʾ (T)	ض Ḍād
ي Yāʾ (Y)	و Wāw (W)	ه Hāʾ (H)	ن Nūn (N)	م Mīm (M)	ل Lām (L)	ك Kāf (K)

Note to parents: the Arabic alphabet

It initially consists of 28 letters and is written horizontally from right to left. The shapes of the letters may change depending on the position in the sentence. But the ultimate goal of this picture book is only to introduce the Arabic language to your children in a playful and fun way.

The pronunciation has been made as easy and simple as possible thanks to the phonetic writing in Latin. Thus, your child will be able to read the words easily without worrying about the real pronunciations which can be a bit complex for his age.

We hope your child will enjoy this book as much as we had the pleasure of making it for you. Do not hesitate to leave us your opinion on the Amazon page. Thank you very much.

AT THE FARM

Sheep
خروف - Kharouf

Horse
حصان - Hisan

Rooster
ديك - Diik

Goat
معزة - Maeza

Donkey
حمار - Himar

Chick
كتكوت - Katakut

Hen
دجاجة - Dajaja

Cow
بقرة - Baqara

Duck
بطة - Batta

IN THE FOREST

Bear
دب - Doub

Owl
بومة - Bouma

Fox
ثعلب - Thaelab

Snail
حلزون - Halazoun

Wolf
ذئب - Dhiib

Squirrel
سنجاب - Sinjab

Hedgehog
قنفذ - Qounfod

AT THE ZOO

Elephant
فيل - Fil

Lion
أسد - Asad

Monkey
قرد - Qird

Dolphin
دولفين - Doulfin

Tiger
نمر - Namir

Parrot
ببغاء - Babagha

Giraffe
زرافة - Zarafa

Crocodile
تمساح - Timsah

IN THE DESERT

Dromedary
ناقة - **Naqa**

Scorpio
عقرب - **Aaqrab**

Snake
ثعبان - **Thueban**

Spider
عنكبوت - **Aankabout**

Gazelle
غزال - **Ghazal**

Camel
جمل - **Jamal**

Lizard
سحلية - **Sihlia**

OTHER ANIMALS ...

Cat
Qit - قط

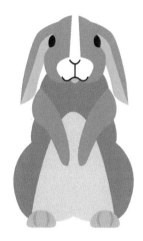

Rabbit
أرنب - Arnab

Fish
سمكة - Samaka

Mouse
فأر - Far

Turtle
سلحفاة - Soulahfat

Dog
كلب - Kalb

FRUITS

Watermelon
بطيخ - Batikh

Ananas
أناناس - Ananas

Raspberry
توت - Tout

Pear
إجاص - Ijjas

Kiwi
كيوي - Kiiwi

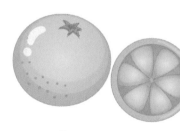

Orange
برتقال - Bortuqal

Lemon
ليمونة - Layamuna

Grape
عنب - Aaynab

Clementine
كليمنتين - Kalimantin

Cherry
كرز - Karaz

FRUITS

Avocado

أفوكادو - Afukadu

Apricot

مشمش - Michmich

Apple

تفاحة - Toffaha

Fig

تين - Tayn

Pomegranate

رمانة - Rommana

Bananas

موز - Mawz

Melon

بطيخ أصفر - Batikh asfar

Strawberry

فراولة - Farawla

Peach

خوخ - Khokh

Link the names in Arabic

أفوكادو	ليمونة	موز	كرز	فراولة
Afukadu	Layamuna	Mawz	Karaz	Farawla

VEGETABLES

Tomato
طماطم - Tamatem

Potato
بطاطس - Batates

Carrot
جزر - Jazar

Turnip
لفت - Lift

Cauliflower
قرنبيط - Qarnabit

Mushroom
فطر - Fotr

Onion
بصلة - Basala

Salad
خس - Khas

Corn
ذرة - Dhora

VEGETABLES

Pepper
فلفل - **Filfil**

Garlic
ثوم - **Toum**

Broccoli
بروكلي - **Barukli**

Aubergine
باذنجان - **Badhinjan**

Pumpkin
يقطين - **Yaqtin**

Courgette
كوسة - **Kosa**

Artichoke
خرشوف - **Kharchouf**

Cucumber
خيار - **Khiar**

Green bean
فاصوليا خضراء
Fasolia khadra

FOOD

Salad
سلطة - **Salata**

Chocolate
شوكولاتة - **Chukulata**

Milk
حليب - **Halib**

Honey
عسل - **Easal**

Egg
بيضة - **Bayda**

Candy
حلوة - **Halwa**

Cookie
بسكويت - **Baskawit**

Cake
كعكة - **Kaeka**

Bread
رغيف الخبز
Raghif alkhubz

MEANS OF TRANSPORT

Car
Sayyara - سيارة

Bus
Haafila - حافلة

Ambulance
Sayarat 'iiseaf - سياره اسعاف

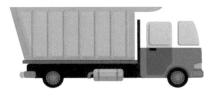

Truck
Shahinat naql - شاحنة نقل

Train
Qitar - قطار

Taxi
Sayarat ojrah - سيارة اجره

Motorbike
Darraja naria - دراجة نارية

Bicycle
Darraja - دراجة

MEANS OF TRANSPORT

Boat
قارب - Qarib

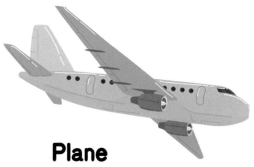

Plane
طائرة - Tayira

Tractor
جرار - Jarrar

Helicopter
حوامة - Hawwama

Rocket
صاروخ - Sarukh

MUSIC

Violin
Kaman - كمان

Guitar
Ghytar - غيتار

Tam-tam
Tamtam - طمطم

Piano
Bianu - بيانو

Xylophone
'iiksilifun - إكسيليفون

Saxophone
Saxofon - سكسفون

Accordion
Akurdiyun - أكورديون

SPORT

Football

Kourat alqadam - كرة القدم

Basketball

Kourat Assala - كرة السلة

Tennis

Tinis - تنس

Tennis table

Tinis attawila - تنس الطاولة

Swimming

Sibaha - سباحة

Cycling

Rukub aldirajat - ركوب الدراجات

AT SCHOOL

Pencil

قلم رصاص - **Qalam rasas**

Notebook

دفتر - **Daftar**

Scissors

مقص - **Miqas**

Book

كتاب - **Kitab**

Schoolbag

محفظة - **Mihfada**

Pen

قلم - **Qalam**

Rule

مسطرة - **Mistara**

Painting

صباغة - **Sibagha**

Paintbrush

فرشاة - **Furchaat**

Board سبورة - Sabboura

The teacher
أستاد - Oustad

The boy
ولد - Walad

The girl
بنت - Bint

House بيت - Bayt

IN THE LIVING ROOM AND BEDROOM

Armchair
كنبة - Kanaba

Television
تلفاز - Tilfaz

Chair
كرسي - Korsi

Sofa
أريكة - Arika

Table
طاولة - Tawila

Desk
مكتب - Maktab

Bed
سرير - Sarir

THE BATHROOM

Mirror
مرآة - Miraat

Towel
منشفة - Minchafa

Soap
صابون - Saaboun

Bathrobe
لباس حمام
Libas Hammam

Bathtub
حوض - Hawd

Carpet
بساط - Bisaat

Toilets
مرحاض - Mirhad

Toothpaste
معجون أسنان
Maejoun Asnan

Toothbrush
فرشاة أسنان
Fourchat Asnan

Washing machine
غسالة - Ghassala

Toilet paper
ورق الحمام - Waraq alhamam

THE KITCHEN

Fork
شوكة - Chawka

Spoon
ملعقة - Milaaqa

Plate
صحن - Sahn

Bowl
وعاء - Wiaa

Knife
سكين - Sikkine

Mug
كوب - Koub

Cooking pot
طنجرة - Tanjara

Teapot
إبريق - Ibriq

Oven
فرن - Forn

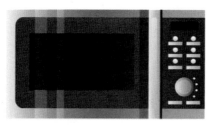

Microwave
فرن كهرباء - Forn kahraba

Saucepan
قدر - Qadr

YELLOW / Asfar
أصفر

Cheese
Jobn - جبن

Moon
Qamar - قمر

Sun
Chams - شمس

Corn
Dhora - ذرة

Bee
Nahla - نحلة

Duck
Batta - بطة

Car
Sayyara - سيارة

Banana
Mawza - موزة

Star
Najma - نجمة

Ananas
Ananas - أناناس

RED / Ahmar
أحمر

Heart
قلب - **Qalb**

Strawberry
فرولة - **Farawla**

Tomato
طماطم - **Tamatem**

Chilli
فلفل حار - **Filfil Har**

Flower
زهرة - **Zahra**

Cherry
كرز - **Karaz**

Watermelon
بطيخ - **Batikh**

GREEN / Akhdar
أخضر

Leaf
Waraqa - ورقة

Avocado
أفوكادو
Afukadu

Apple
تفاحة - Toffaha

Lizard
سحلية - Sihlia

Turtle
سلحفاة - Soulahfat

Tree
شجرة - Chajara

Frog
ضفدع - Difdaa

Worm
دودة - Douda

BLUE / Azraq
أزرق

Cloud
سحابة - **Sahaba**

Bird
عصفور - **Osfour**

Felt
ملون - **Moulawwin**

Drop
قطرة - **Qatra**

Trousers
سروال - **Sirwal**

Butterfly
فراشة - **Faracha**

Fish
سمكة - **Samaka**

ORANGE / Bortuqali
برتقالي

Pumpkin
يقطين - Yaqtin

Juice
عصير - Asiir

Orange
برتقال - Bortuqal

Tiger
نمر - Namir

Bow
عقدة - Oqda

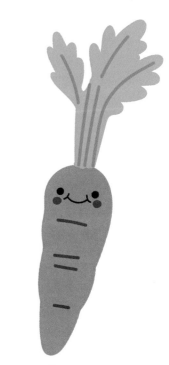

Carrot
جزرة - Jazara

BLACK / Aswad
أسود

Cat
قط - **Qit**

Board
سبورة - **Sabboura**

Wheel
عجلة - **Aajala**

Speaker
سماعة -
Samaa'a

Shoes
حذاء - **Hidae**

Glasses
نظرات - **Nazzarat**

Boots

أحذية - 'ahadhiya

Coconut

جوز هند - Jawz Hind

Cake

كعكة - Kaeka

Coffee

قهوة - Qahwa

Bear

دب - Doub

Ice cream

بوظة - Bouza

Link the colours and their names in Arabic

Akhdar

Azraq

Bortuqali

Ahmar

Asfar

THE FIGURES

1

One
واحد
Wahid

2

Two
إثنان
Ithnan

3

Three
ثلاثة
Thalata

4

Four
أربعة
Arbaa

5

Five
خمسة
Khamsa

6

Six
ستة
Sitta

7

Seven
سبعة
Sabaa

8

Eight
ثمانية
Thamania

9

Nine
تسعة
Tisaa

10

Ten
عشرة
Achara

CLOTHES

T-shirt
قميص - Qamis

Hat
قبعة - Qobea

Slippers
نعال - Neal

Short
تبان - Toubban

Jumper
سترة - Soutra

Trousers
سروال - Sirwal

Boots
أحذية - Ahdia

Cap
قبعة - Qobea

CLOTHES

Skirt
تنورة - Tannoura

Gloves
قفازات - Qaffazat

Trainers
أحذية رياضية - Ahdia riyadiya

Coat
معطف - Meataf

Socks
جوارب - Jawarib

Pyjamas
منامة - Manama

Dress
فستان - Foustan

LINK THE PICTURES AND THEIR NAMES IN ARABIC

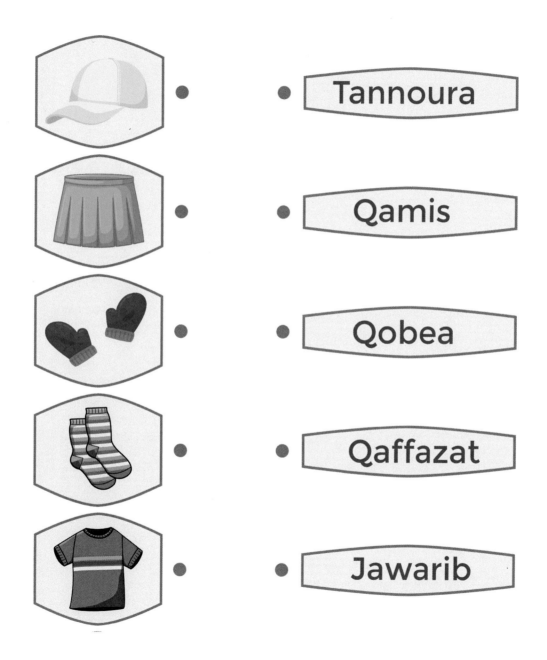

Tannoura

Qamis

Qobea

Qaffazat

Jawarib

THE BODY

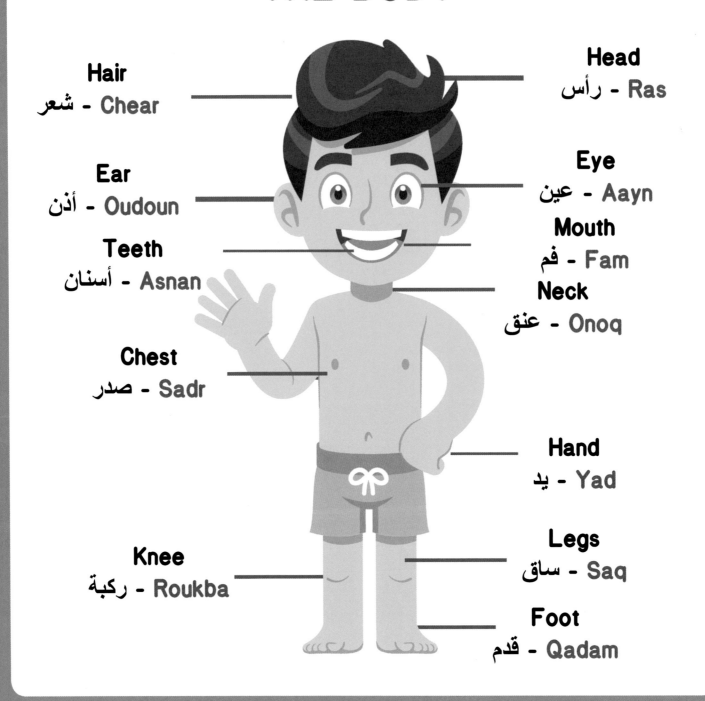

Hair
شعر - Chear

Ear
أذن - Oudoun

Teeth
Asnan - أسنان

Chest
صدر - Sadr

Knee
Roukba - ركبة

Head
رأس - Ras

Eye
Aayn - عين

Mouth
فم - Fam

Neck
Onoq - عنق

Hand
Yad - يد

Legs
Saq - ساق

Foot
Qadam - قدم

THE LABYRINTH GAME

I see
أرى - Ara

THE SEASONS

Spring

ربيع - Rabii

Summer

صيف - Sayf

Autumn

خريف - Kharif

Winter

شتاء - Chitae

THE WEATHER

Sun
شمس - Chams

Moon
قمر - Qamar

Cold
Bard - برد

Hot
Harara - حرارة

Cloudy
Gha'im - غائم

Stars
Noujoum - نجوم

lightning
Barq - برق

Rain
Matar - مطر

Rainbow
Qaws Qozah - قوس قزح

Snow
Thalj - ثلج

Made in the USA
Middletown, DE
12 December 2024

66739161R00024